For Crying Out Loud

Chantelle Pettus

BookLeaf Publishing

India | USA | UK

Presentation by *BookLeaf Publishing*

Web: www.bookleafpub.com

E-mail: info@bookleafpub.com

ISBN: 9789358318968

First edition 2024

*I hear in dedicate this book to the idea of love
and hope. To those whom ever dealt with
depression. Anyone who is ever felt alone and
still chooses to fight everday. You have purpose
and your not alone.*

ACKNOWLEDGEMENT

I'd like to thank my parents james and linda pettus and my two sibblings Jermaine and Shawn you guys helped to create who i am. My four failed relationships helped me gain experience, to know my worth, to know what i do and do not like. Thru the pain and let down ive grown stronger. I appriecate all the English and creative writing teachers and proffersors that gave me incouragement.

PREFACE

Here is a collection of my thoughts, my outlook of life , my fears, desires, struggles, and dreams. Take a peek in my mind. It's very important as a human to be heard, get things off your chest and

ONE DAY

Being with child makes you a lady.
Being without is driving me crazy.
All that's left to say is that one, one day.
One day , someday , one day.

On my hip, by my side, they'll be my joy and
pride, till the day i die. I'll give them all that's
mine .
One day, someday, oneday

Need someone to carry on my legacy.
Teach them all, all that's been taught to me. One
day , some day, one day. One day , some way,
I'll have my baby.

So damn in love

How could i put myself through this again. Why did i put myself into this predicament no no no not again. I'm so in love, i'm so damn in love with you.

Had my heart open let it swing. I tried to fight it, I don't know what to do, I feel so confused. I'm so in love, i'm so damn in love with you.

I know I got to hold myself back , But I just can't help it. I've tried, but my heart just won't hide. How do I live my life?

Why can't I learn how to play this cool? I feel like such a fool. I'm scared i'm really scared i'm so in love, I'm so goddamn in love with you.

New York

New york where its always dark, where the city lights are so bright. Where little kids get into fights, Where you have to be tough where boys get rough with little girls, We're old women get their pearls snatched. We're druggies are catched in board daylight, Where at night? You have to keep your doors locked unless you intend on getting robbed or raped. New York where its gloomy and looney's running muck. Where life just sucks where people just don't give a fuck.

I'm only human

I have a soul, I have a heart. I have feelings I have ideas and fears. It appears that I am only human i'm made out of flesh and blood. I'm also made out of love from above. I made mistakes it aches I bleed when wounded. Do I not or have you forgotten that I am only human . I have a personality. I have a mind that you can define if you take the time to find out that I am only human.

Can I rest now

Don't really know how to describe these feelings, Don't know how to express myself without seeming morbid. Except that I can't close my eyes without thinking about what I don't have. I don't want to be alone, I don't wanna be lonely old maid, And I cringe and cry at the thought. I try to stop myself from thinking of it. Try to stop the fears but they dominate. I'm terrified at the thought of this. Scares me to know and whats worst I fear I have no control over them as I would like. I feel useless pointless to exist unneeded I am not a necessity. Sure i'm a daughter, sure i'm a sister and an aunt but what I am i really? What am I really needed for not to be a mother apparently. Doomed not to be anyone's lover, someone's everything, who am i? Someone please tell me. It may seem crazy but I say to myself. I want to go home,where am I? I am home but it doesn't feel like it. Maybe I am crazy but just maybe I'm not supposed to be here anymore. These man-made cliche's are not helping. Your day will come. You're still young.

I believe myself to be patient. However I don't
want to wait through this pain anymore. There's
only so much I can tolerate.
This is not self-pity.
Not for anyone's objections or understandings. I
just want my pain to end. I know whatever I
think to do would be a quick would stop my
mortal pain. But then what there's the scary part?
What if I succeed at this task will my pain really
stop? And will I be in a better place? What if my
happy ending or intended happiness was on its
way and I just didn't wait long enough.
I just want to know when I can rest. Can I
please rest now?
Is all the pain going to end so I can rest can I rest
now?

I still can

Still can taste your kiss. I really do miss you.
Why do I feel like a fool for even trusting in
you? But there's nothing I can do. Still can see
flashbacks of you and me and what we used to
be. I thought you were my one and only. How
could this be? How could I believe.
I thought you was it, but I guess I was wrong.
Still got plenty of love for you, and it's still very
strong. Still can feel your tender touch. You
know I miss you so much. You passionate graze
still amazes me. Can't you see I need you near
me.
Still can smell the roses you gave me, smell The
bottle of cologne I bought you.
Still can hear your whisper sweet nothings damn
why you had to go and kiss her. Trying to sweet
talk yourself into my heart and it worked.
I can now say honestly I was blind. Always
gonna remember all the time we shared. But I
think back and still wonder if you cared. Just
remember that I will always be here.
Still can imagine a future. I'll still hold out hope.
Because that's one thing nobody can take for me.
I still can believe in whatever I want to believe.

Rain

Looking out the glass window, misty foggy,
frosty with water vapor. the smell of wet Earth
and wet dog from letting the canine in the house.
the smell of ocean mist. The cars ride by splish
splash a big splat on the sidewalk.
It's like the night or day has feelings, for a rainy
day it's lonely, sad and depressed. Into a shape of
a little drop as it drips down the window seal.
You can almost hear moaning and sighing of the
young girl.
Which can be mistaken for the hectic wind
whirling around. The heavens are crying. Tear
drops fall onto my head as I walk along the
lonely streets. Swept up by the stream of grief.
Rain it nurtures the earth and ground. I
sometimes love the sound. Bitter sweet it washes
away the bad and brings good up to surface. I
wish the rain could wash away my pain.

Tired

As she smokes her cigarette inhaling quickly and heavily now slowly and deeply. As of now, her once rapid heartbeat is now a slow and steady pump. Her heart pumps slower and slower and slower. She day dreams of a beautiful land or life. Repeatedly in my mind so tired, so tired, so very tired. Must get rest as her eyes shut, she doesn't fight it. She drifts further and further and further away.
Somewhere pleasant and happy place. She enters somewhere at peace and of relaxation tender touchs of warmth. "Hey, are you with us? Where'd you go" a girl says I counted to 3. 1...2....3 ....I open my eyes huh "what you say?"

Don't come back to me

You want to go out and play? You wanna go have it your way? Wanna go out in the street's boy don't come home to me. That's fine with me don't come back in my sheets.
Do what you wanna do, but don't expect me to stay at home and wait for you. You can do what you like even spend the night. You can have what you like any cake and any pie But you won't have mine what's on your mind.
When you wanna come home to me don't come back to me. You won't get your cake and eat it too. Wanna go out act a fool don't come back to me.

Emotions

I want to cry over the past pain that left me in shame. I want to cry over the happiness of my present that I did gain. Can't believe the Bliss I've sustained, got me jumping and running through the rain. I don't even believe the darkness that I have overcome just wanted to tell the world I've won shout it yell, it scream it out loud. Yeah, found my happiness again. That's so many emotions they overwhelmed me. Life got me singing again even if it's off key not saying s*** is perfect. I'm just saying I'm happy now and I deserve it. Dancing more than I ever did before? Can't stop these feet from moving across the floor of emotions. Twisting to the beat of life never again will I fear defeat,that wouldn't happen twice but no regrets. I wouldn't dull any of my emotions for the world. I will always seek out and conquer any emotion that comes my way because without them I am no one.

Can I get back to me

It's been so long that I had to think about what I
need. Can even tell how many times I've been on
my knees literally. When people ask what I want
and what makes me happy all that I see is what
used to be, but then I realized that's dead and
gone. Then I feel in the room for loving
yourself. Strong. How do I get back to me
It's not a floor that I love so strong. All the love
that I display, I don't really regret, but that's the
only way I know how but can I get back to me
somehow, some way somebody, please tell me,
is it possible to find yourself after loving
someone else? The soldier, I'm alone, what's
going on, I don't know what to do. Now that we
are through, don't know what I need for how to
make myself happy.
What it is that I want. Don't know how to give it
a thoubut what? But what makes my world go
round? Is making someone else happy. So I'm
gonna give this love thing one more try. So I can
get back to me. I'll find My Way. I'll do it one
day trust and believe I can get back to me.

Misdeal

I'm calling it a miss deal, are you for real? This is how it works. Why do good things happen to bad people? And why do bad things happen to good people? The aint right this ain't fun giving me a cheap shot and life's only begun.
The cards that I'm dealt, how I felt so cheated. Want to give him back, see where I'd be at. This shit is rough called life. I'm calling the dealers bluff. Call it what you want. It's a cheesy shot, a low blow, take it back Re shuffle I'm calling a misdeal on life.

Reflection

As she looks at a reflection in the mirror. they say I saw the windows to the soul. If so her soul is clouded and shadowed. she can't see her own pupils from the raining of her heart. As her eyes redden and the tear ducks overflow with overwhelming emotion The reflection cries out what is wrong with you.
Could it be the wrinkle of your nose when you cry? Could it be the honey brown glitz of your eyes? When they're wet with tears? Could it be the soft twitching your lip? When emotions are flowing, maybe not, but still. This woman is a flower with no roots. A predator with no prey, the glove without a hand or purpose. If any is well hidden.. she used to look at the reflection in sea life. Love happiness because she was looking through 2 sets of eyes. Now that she has lost the other set of eyes, she cries because she cannot see. She had 2 sets along and in the last one. She's in pain because she can't breathe, she had 2 hearts. But now one is gone. She's done because now she can't go on. She now screams at the reflection. I can't see I can't breathe, can't live! You see I've lost my other parts reflection says silly "They were extra parts. I know you've

grown attached, but you are made without. So you'll do fine until we find You some more parts."

Perfect

My heart is as deeper as all the Earth sea's. And the greatest thing is that there is no feast to pay to have my heart. All I want is you near my love. Stretches further than all the Earth's atmosphere. My soul is brighter than all the universe. Son's combined. I should have my own Shawn, but there is too many takers. My my aura is as beautiful as seeing and guardian angel or our maker. In this world, there is not enough givers. Selfishness is the disease that is so hard to overcome but believe me. You may take take what you're not one because you can love yourself. But you've got to learn to love someone else. I know this lesson all too well. And since I'm this beautiful inside and out One day I'll meet my perfect spouse.

Don't leave me

Hold me, kiss me. Tell me you love me. I'll stomp my feet I'll scream ill scream don't leave me always be with me.

Tell me boy what a girl gotta do to be kick. Do I gotta scream and gotta play these silly games? Shouldn't be this hard boy, you've got me scared. Can imagine life without you don't be a fool. You know, I love you and I hope you feel the same way as i do.

They say you don't know what you got to look school and but sometimes they're wrong, I knew what I had I was just so stupid. I know I'm a good woman and you're a good man. But if we can make this work I know this can be so good. I know deep down in my heart that you were meant for me. And this is meant to be so don't leave me if we can get over all the obstacles and be in control. Over our destiny, I know I love congrowing. Bro and go on to a new level of love.

This love is very special. I know you love me and I love you. But when it gets hard and we don't know what to do. Just don't throw in the towel we gotta fight for all it's worth.

This love is worth a whole lot cause I got you back and you got mine Fava. Don't waste anymore. Time come home and be mine don't leave me.

Time

Time files by, hold on to it, grip it with dear life
for it runs away from you. Time is of the
essence it has an unspoken contract that none of
knows when expires all. Societal time plays
tricks with the mind ,it makes you think that
your behind in a race though that may not even
be the case. Time goes so quick one second
your lively and thriving and the next your sick.
Who made these rules of time, we were doing
just fine without it. We are fools and slaves to
the clock as it says tic toc our anxitey, patience,
and depression sets in. Time waits for no one, it
doesn't care if you are dying, crying , working,
or twerking.
 I find there's never enough time. No matter
what I do I feel left behind and its so hard to
look forward when you feel like you've forgotten
something in the past. Time you evil creation my
biological clock hates you. I should have
finished schooling earlier, I should have been
wed by now, I should have my life together by
now. The shoulda, woulda, coulda of time
infests my mind.
    All those whom had loved ones who seemed
to be taken too soon detest you time. You show

no mercy, all we want is a little bit more of you,
you move too soon. There is never enough of
you, it's a cruel game you play on all of us. Time
is not on my side, time I can actually hear you
slipping away like a bandit in the night.

Time there's no plea I can make, if its
someone's time you will take. If its meant in
your moment you will show it. You are never
enough time!

No care

You say you love me. You say you care, but why aren't you? There? Nights are cold not from the weather, but from my despair. Depression creeps inside me takes over like a parasite.
It was my control down a lover. That's also my best friend. Where'd you go when I needed you? Why did you not come back to save me? You we're my world, thoughts of your well being was always on my mind
except when it was time to check on me, you didn't.
I was digging myself out of my own grave and you put me there. Without a second thought. I was a problem that you couldn't be bothered with sex. There was no night in Charlie Marlin rescue me. Ask me again if I believe you cared for me.

Stuck

I'm stuck in a country mudhole without two
wheel drive and nobody around for miles. I'm
stuck on the side of a mountain with an
ambulance. Approaching buried multiple yards
deep with slim chances I'll survive. I'm stuck in
a well with no Lassie nearby.I'm trapped in a
garbage room disposal with wolves coming in
and no. I'm trapped in a cave with rocks
tumbling Creating a caven when hopes for a
search party are bleak. I'm sinking to the bottom
of the ocean with brickside to my feet with no
dreams of getting free and call didi. I'm trapped
in nightmare with a killer on my tail racing to a
door that will not allow me to exit with no hero
to save me.
I'm stuck in quick sand of a fire swamp thinking
more and more with no resources in the side. I'm
trapped in the air tight container bunker. Win
ventilation stools. stuck in a submarine
thousands of feet below. When it begins to take
on water and no emergency guideline strategies.
Paralyzed by fear of stuck realization of the
inevitable i'm stuck. Drained by hopelessness, I
sank exhausted by helplessness. I'm stuck trying
to fight that inevitable is useless. and escape is

what I must find, but how can you escape when
you're stuck within your own mind.

Panic

Those dreadful words, deal breaking words that literally break my heart. No budge in you, no compromise, told me what i dare not hear. With three failed relationships, no hope to have a child now because you stomped my dream out. I drive along the friendship path and drop you off to go about your day as if nothing happened. I don't make it very far before what feels like an earthquake erupts inside of my body. Sobbing uncontrollablly and hyperventilating , all i wanted was a baby and my dream was gone he took it from me. It was very hard to see, I pulled on the side of the road. Because I knew I could not control the vehicle with this earthquake shaking my very core. I reach for my phone to call a life line and i notice my hands shaking so hard i can barely hold the phone. I struggle to punch buttons or numbers. The shrill and shreaks that came from my mouth i can imagine were unrecognizable to the party on the other end of the receiver when I finally got my hands stable enough to dial out. I sat there for a while contemplating, and trying to fight off this hopeless feeling. I was defeated by my ideal life disappearing in front of my eyes . I had no

wounds that the eye can see, no broken bones ,
no blood dripping. Did i just have a panic attack
or was i tripping?